Tanka's Tender Touch

Unveiling Emotional Depth Through Concise Verse

Brennan Fairchild

Contents

Contents

1 Introduction: The Art of Tanka
Chapter 1: Understanding Form

The tanka, a Japanese poetic form, is deceptively simple in its structure: five lines containing a precise syllable count—five, seven, five, seven, and seven syllables, respectively. This seemingly rigid framework, however, is the very foundation of its power. It demands economy of language, forcing the poet to select words with surgical precision, each syllable carrying significant weight. Mastering this structure is the first step towards unlocking the tanka's potential for expressing profound emotions and evocative imagery. Consider the difference between a rambling narrative and a tightly crafted haiku; the tanka, bridging the gap, allows for more nuanced storytelling within its concise form. Understanding the syllable count isn't just about counting; it's about feeling the rhythm, the pulse of the poem, and how that rhythm contributes to its overall impact.

Beyond the numerical structure, the essence of a compelling tanka lies in its ability to evoke vivid imagery. This is often achieved through the skillful use of kigo, seasonal words that act as anchors, grounding the poem in a specific time and place. A single kigo—a blossoming cherry tree, the chirping of crickets, the first snowfall—can transport the reader to a particular season, instantly establishing a mood and context. Imagine the difference between simply stating "it's cold" and describing "frost clinging to withered leaves," the latter invoking a far richer sensory experience. The use of kigo isn't just about naming seasons; it's about harnessing their inherent symbolic power to enhance the emotional resonance of the poem. These words act as keys, unlocking layers of meaning and allowing the poet to convey complex feelings through subtle suggestion rather than explicit declaration. Precise word choice is paramount in tanka. Each word must earn its place, contributing to the overall effect. Avoid clichés and overly general terms; strive for specificity and concreteness. Think about the power of strong verbs and evocative nouns—words that paint pictures in the reader's mind. Consider the impact of sensory details: the texture of a worn wooden floor, the scent of rain on hot pavement, the sound of waves crashing against the shore. These details bring the poem to life, creating an immersive experience for the reader. Remember that brevity necessitates precision; every word must work harmoniously with the others, creating a unified and powerful whole. The beauty of tanka lies in its ability to convey immense emotional depth through a restrained, almost minimalist approach.

The arrangement of words and phrases within the five lines is crucial. The careful placement of line breaks can control the rhythm and pace of the poem, guiding the reader's attention and shaping their understanding of the poem's meaning. A short line can create a sense of pause, reflection, or sudden revelation. A longer line can build momentum, creating a sense of flow and continuity. Experiment with different line breaks to see how they affect the overall feeling of the poem. This is where the art of the tanka truly reveals itself; it is more than just a numerical exercise; it's a dance of words and rhythm, carefully choreographed to produce a harmonious and emotionally resonant effect. Think of the lines as musical phrases, each contributing to the overall melody of the poem.

Finally, remember the iterative nature of the creative process. The first draft is rarely the final product. Revise your work relentlessly. Refine word choices, experiment with line breaks, and consider the poem's overall impact. Seek feedback from trusted readers, but trust your own intuition. The most important aspect of writing a tanka, or any poem for that matter, is to create a work that resonates with you and speaks to your heart. Remember: the tanka is a small vessel capable of carrying a vast emotional ocean. The mastery of its form unlocks the potential to express profound emotions and experiences in a way that is both poignant and unforgettable. Through careful attention to detail and a commitment to revision, you can harness the power of the tanka and create poems that are both beautiful and meaningful.

1.1   Syllable Structure

The five-syllable structure of the tanka is its defining characteristic, yet understanding its nuances is key to mastering the form. It's not merely a count; it's a rhythm, a breath, a carefully constructed miniature world contained within its concise framework. Each syllable carries weight; it contributes to the overall flow and impact of the poem. Consider how a single misplaced syllable can disrupt the delicate balance, altering the intended mood or meaning. Precise syllable count enhances the elegance and subtlety crucial to the tanka's effect.

Think of the tanka as a musical phrase, each syllable a note, contributing to the overall melody. A perfectly counted tanka sings; a slightly off-kilter one falters. The consistent syllable structure provides a framework, a scaffold upon which the poet builds their emotional architecture. This structure encourages precision and concision, forcing the poet to choose each word carefully, maximizing its impact within the limited space. This discipline sharpens the poet's awareness of language's power. Think of each syllable as a brushstroke in a miniature painting, where every stroke contributes to the final image.

Mastering the five-syllable structure isn't about rigid adherence to rules; it's about understanding the underlying principle of balance and harmony. Think about how the different lengths of the lines—five, seven, five, seven, seven—create a natural rhythm, guiding the reader's eye and ear through the poem. This inherent rhythm is a powerful tool; it allows for subtle shifts in pacing, building suspense or creating moments of quiet reflection. Experiment with the flow, noticing how the rhythmic pattern enhances the meaning you wish to convey. The rhythm itself becomes another layer of meaning, weaving itself into the emotional tapestry of the poem.

The precision demanded by the tanka's syllable structure ultimately leads to greater clarity and impact. It encourages poets to choose words deliberately, eliminating unnecessary words and focusing on those that carry the most weight. This precision forces a distillation of thought and emotion, allowing for powerful and poignant expressions even in such brevity. This contrasts the often-verbose nature of longer poetic forms. The conciseness inherent in the tanka's form isn't about limiting expression but sharpening it, making it more potent, more memorable.

Furthermore, consider the cultural context. The tanka, originating in Japan, developed its structure over centuries. The structure itself has a history, echoing cultural values and aesthetic preferences. While we may not fully understand all of its historical nuances, being aware of the form's heritage provides a deeper appreciation for its artistry and precision. Understanding the historical context adds another layer to your understanding and enhances your creative process.

To truly master the tanka's syllable structure, practice is vital. Begin by counting syllables in existing tankas, paying close attention to how different poets utilize the form. Then, try writing your own five-syllable lines, focusing on the rhythm and flow. Don't be afraid to experiment with different word choices, exploring how slight changes affect the overall impact. Practice helps to internalize the structure, allowing you to write naturally and intuitively while adhering to the form's constraints.

Finally, remember that the syllable structure is not merely a technical requirement but a fundamental element shaping the emotional impact of your tanka. It's the foundation upon which you build your poetic world, allowing the inherent rhythm to underscore and enhance the emotions you convey. By truly mastering this structure, you unlock the tanka's potent ability to communicate profound emotions within a remarkably concise and beautiful form. It's a journey of refinement and discovery, a dance between constraint and creative freedom, resulting in a poetry form that is simultaneously structured and free, precise and evocative.

1.2   Kigo & Imagery

The heart of tanka, its vibrant pulse, lies in the kigo, the seasonal word. This isn't merely a descriptive term; it's a portal, transporting the reader to a specific time and place, evoking a sensory experience so potent it resonates long after the poem ends. Imagine, for instance, "winter's first snow," a simple phrase, yet it conjures up a world of imagery: the hushed silence of a freshly fallen landscape, the crisp air biting at exposed skin, the soft crunch of footsteps on pristine white. This single kigo can anchor an entire tanka, providing a foundation upon which the poet builds layers of emotional resonance.

Consider the difference between saying "a flower blooms" and "cherry blossoms unfurl in spring's gentle breeze." The first is generic, lacking the specificity and emotional depth of the second. The kigo, "cherry blossoms," instantly grounds the image in a precise moment, suggesting themes of renewal, fragility, and the ephemeral beauty of life. It invites the reader to participate, to recall personal experiences connected with spring, blossoms, and the subtle shift in the natural world.

Mastering the kigo is crucial for crafting effective tanka. It's not about simply listing seasonal elements; rather, it involves carefully selecting words that resonate deeply with the poem's central emotion. A kigo that feels forced or irrelevant will weaken the tanka, detracting from its overall impact. It needs to be a harmonious addition, enriching the overall meaning and feeling. It takes practice and a sensitivity to the nuances of language.

Effective imagery, working hand-in-hand with the kigo, is another vital component of successful tanka. The goal is not mere description, but the evocation of feeling. Consider the difference between "the sun shone brightly" and "the sun, a molten coin, spilled gold across the fields." The latter employs a metaphor, creating a vivid, memorable image that engages multiple senses. It appeals not just to sight, but also to the feeling of warmth and the richness of the color gold. It's in these choices that the poet can add layers of meaning and make the imagery far more affecting.

To enhance imagery, try engaging all five senses. Don't just describe what you see, but also the sounds, smells, tastes, and textures associated with the kigo and the poem's theme. This creates a more immersive and emotionally engaging experience for the reader. Imagine the faint scent of plum blossoms in a spring rain, or the sound of cicadas buzzing in the summer heat. These sensory details bring the tanka to life, making it more than just words on a page.

Remember, the beauty of tanka lies in its brevity. Every word counts; every image must serve a purpose. Resist the urge to overcrowd your poems with unnecessary details. Instead, focus on creating sharp, concise images that convey your emotions effectively. The key is to use carefully chosen words and imagery that create a powerful emotional impact on the reader.

Finally, don't be afraid to experiment. The beauty of tanka is its capacity for capturing a wealth of emotion and ideas within such a small framework. Use vivid language to communicate the feelings you want your readers to feel and consider how other writers use imagery to achieve specific results. Embrace the inherent constraints of the form as a source of creativity, allowing them to shape your ideas in unexpected and rewarding ways. Through careful selection of kigo and precise imagery, you can craft tanka that are both technically masterful and deeply moving. Let the natural world speak through your words, letting your poetry take root and blossom in their own time.

2 Chapter 2: Exploring Themes

Love and loss, a potent combination, frequently explored within the concise framework of the tanka. Think of the fleeting nature of romance, the sharp sting of heartbreak, or the quiet ache of remembrance. Consider Basho's masterful exploration of loss, his poems often imbued with a poignant serenity. He captures the essence of absence, not with dramatic pronouncements but with subtle details, a fallen blossom, an empty teacup, conveying a depth of emotion that resonates far beyond the poem's brevity. This subtle approach allows the reader to actively participate in completing the meaning, drawing from their own experiences to fully understand the depth of feeling. We find that the most effective tankas on love and loss don't explicitly state the emotion, but rather imply it through imagery and carefully chosen words.

Nature's embrace, another prevalent theme, offers boundless inspiration. The changing seasons, the vibrant colors of autumn leaves, the stark beauty of a winter landscape—these offer a plethora of sensory details to weave into your tankas. The Japanese aesthetic, deeply connected to the natural world, provides a rich foundation for exploring this theme. Observe closely. Really see the details. The delicate dance of snowflakes, the rugged strength of a mountain, the vibrant energy of a spring meadow. Each holds a potential story, waiting to be unlocked within the precise structure of a tanka. Consider the power of kigo, seasonal words, to instantly ground the poem in a specific time and place, enhancing the emotional impact of your work. A simple cherry blossom, for instance, can evoke an entire season of hope, renewal, and the bittersweet passage of time.

The spiritual quest, a theme that speaks to the human desire for meaning and connection, provides a profound wellspring for poetic expression. This doesn't necessarily necessitate overt religious references; instead, consider moments of introspection, reflection on the human condition, or the search for truth and understanding. A tanka, with its concise structure, can capture the essence of a spiritual experience with remarkable economy. Think of the feeling of awe inspired by a vast night sky, the peace found in solitude, or the sense of wonder at the interconnectedness of all things. These experiences, often deeply personal, can translate into powerful and moving poems when conveyed with honesty and sensitivity. Remember, your unique perspective and personal journey are invaluable assets. Don't be afraid to explore your inner world; your authenticity will shine through in your work. The spiritual quest is a journey, and your tankas can reflect the stages, the doubts, and the moments of revelation along the way. Let your poem mirror the depth and complexity of your own inner landscape. Each of these themes—love and loss, nature's embrace, and the spiritual quest—offers a unique opportunity to explore the depths of human emotion within the limited space of a tanka. Mastering the art of suggestion, of hinting at rather than explicitly stating, is key to creating resonant and evocative poems. The challenge lies in selecting the most potent images and words to convey the intended emotion without being overly descriptive or verbose. This requires careful observation, mindful reflection, and a willingness to experiment with language. The seemingly simple structure of the tanka serves as a crucible, forging powerful emotional experiences through the careful selection and arrangement of words. It's about precision, not quantity, about resonance, not detail. The most impactful tankas are often those that leave the reader with more questions than answers, prompting contemplation and further reflection.

2.1   Love & Loss

The heart aches, a familiar rhythm, a dull thud against the ribs. Loss, a shadow stretching long across the sunlit fields of memory. It whispers of laughter shared, of hands clasped, of promises made under a sky brimming with stars. Those memories, once vibrant and sharp, now softened by the passage of time, yet their essence remains. We cling to these fragments, the echoes of what was, building a fragile raft to navigate the turbulent waters of grief. The pain, sharp initially, gradually mellows, becoming a persistent undercurrent in the flow of daily life. This isn't forgetting, but an acceptance, a quiet understanding that the love remains, transformed, etched into the very fabric of our being.

It's a different kind of love now, a quiet strength born from sorrow. The laughter still echoes, but it's tinged with a wistful melancholy. There's a sacred space carved within the heart, a sanctuary dedicated to remembrance; a testament to a bond that time cannot erase. This is not a negation of the loss itself, but the beginning of a transformation. The initial shock gives way to reflection. Memories, once jagged shards, become smoothed pebbles, carefully collected and cherished. The pain transforms, shaping and molding the soul. We are altered, indelibly marked by the imprint of loss, but not broken. The love, woven into the tapestry of our lives, endures.

Consider the tanka as a mirror reflecting these intricacies of emotion. Its brevity demands precision, forcing us to select only the most potent words, the most poignant images to convey the depth of our feelings. A single line, carefully crafted, can evoke a cascade of emotions – the sting of separation, the quiet ache of longing, the tenacious hold of memory. Through the careful selection of kigo, the seasonal references can amplify the feeling. The falling leaves of autumn, mirroring the slow decay of a relationship, or the persistent bloom of a spring flower, hinting at the enduring power of love that transcends even death.

The simplicity of the form is deceptive. Within its five lines lies an immense capacity for conveying nuance and emotional complexity. Each syllable carries weight, each word a carefully chosen brushstroke on the canvas of the heart. In writing about love and loss, we are not simply recounting events, but exploring the profound inner landscape of our emotions, the shifting terrain of the human spirit. To master this requires not only skill in crafting a concise poem but a deep engagement with our memories, with our grief, with our love.

Writing a tanka about loss isn't merely an exercise in poetic technique; it's an act of catharsis, a way of processing the intensity of our emotions, giving voice to the unspoken. The concise structure of the tanka demands this emotional distillation, forcing us to be precise in our descriptions and deeply intentional in our image selections. The poem itself becomes a conduit, leading to a deeper understanding and acceptance of the experience. This is perhaps its greatest power: to articulate that which defies words, to bring clarity to the chaos of grief.

Begin by focusing on a specific memory. Recall a significant detail – the scent of their perfume, the sound of their laughter, the feel of their hand in yours. Let this single sensory detail serve as the foundation of your tanka. Then, build around it, adding layers of emotion and imagery, each carefully chosen to amplify the core memory. Avoid clichés and generic phrasing; strive for originality and emotional honesty. The power of your poem lies in its authenticity, its ability to resonate with genuine feeling.

Don't strive for perfection, but for honesty. Let the words flow from the heart, untamed and unfiltered. Revision will come later, but initially, focus on capturing the raw emotion, the unvarnished truth of your experience. Let the tanka be a vessel to hold your grief, to honor your love, to acknowledge the profound impact of loss on your life. The process of writing itself becomes an act of healing, a journey towards acceptance, and a testament to the enduring power of love in the face of death. The final poem, however imperfect, stands as a monument to a love that transcends time.

2.2 Nature's Embrace

The whispering wind carries secrets through the tall grasses, secrets only the attentive ear can grasp. Nature, in its vastness, provides an endless wellspring for tanka. Observe the delicate dance of a butterfly on a sundrenched bloom, the silent strength of a towering oak weathering a storm, the hushed reverence of a snow-covered landscape. Each scene, each element, holds a potential narrative, a whispered poem waiting to be born. Let your heart be open to these subtle narratives. Embrace the quiet power of the natural world, for within its rhythms and cycles lies a profound connection to the human spirit. Find inspiration not just in the grand vistas, but in the minute details – the dewdrop clinging to a spider's web, the intricate pattern of a fallen leaf.

Consider the way the sun paints the sky in hues of fiery orange and soft lavender at sunset. How can this fleeting beauty be captured in the concise form of the tanka? Focus on sensory details: the cool evening air on your skin, the scent of damp earth, the distant call of a bird. These specifics will ground your tanka, making it more evocative and personal. Don't be afraid to explore the emotional undercurrents of the natural world, the quiet melancholy of a winter landscape, the joyful exuberance of spring's rebirth. These mirroring emotions within the natural world allow for the expression of deeply personal feelings within your writing.

Imagine the rugged beauty of a mountain range, its peaks piercing the sky. The vastness of such a landscape can be overwhelming, yet the tanka's constraint can help you isolate a specific element – the wind whistling through a rocky pass, the tenacious growth of a pine tree clinging to a cliff face. By focusing on a single detail, you can create a microcosm of the larger scene, a powerful image resonating with the reader's own experiences of nature's awe-inspiring power. Find ways to evoke the feeling of vastness, the sense of scale, without overwhelming your five lines. Less is more.

The ocean, a powerful symbol of both creation and destruction, offers a rich tapestry of imagery for your tanka. Consider the rhythmic crash of waves against the shore, the hypnotic sway of seaweed, the myriad creatures hidden beneath the surface. Think about the ocean's moods – the serene calm of a summer's day, the tempestuous fury of a storm. These varied moods can serve as powerful metaphors for the emotional complexities of the human experience. Let the rhythm of the waves inspire the rhythm of your lines. The ebb and flow can mirror the ebbs and flows of your own feelings.

A solitary tree standing in a vast field presents a powerful symbol of resilience and solitude. Focus on the way the wind bends its branches, the texture of its bark, the birds that nest within its leaves. The image, though simple, can evoke a profound sense of connection to the natural world and the human condition. Consider the subtle interplay between the tree and its environment, the way it stands strong against the elements. This can symbolize human perseverance or isolation, depending on your intention. Explore such themes as acceptance of the harsh realities, and the quiet dignity in facing solitude.

Remember that nature is not just a source of pretty pictures; it's a source of profound emotions and complex ideas. Your tanka doesn't need to be overly descriptive; it needs to evoke feeling. Therefore, it's crucial to connect with your subject matter on an emotional level, to allow your own feelings and perceptions to shape your words. Allow the beauty and power of the natural world to inspire you, to guide your hand as you craft your tanka. Let nature inform your voice.

2.3   Spiritual Quest

The human spirit, a boundless ocean, often seeks solace in the vast expanse of the unknown. This yearning, this spiritual quest, finds poignant expression in the compact form of the tanka. Unlike sprawling epics, the tanka's brevity forces a distillation of feeling, mirroring the focused intensity of spiritual seeking. Think of the quiet contemplation of a monk, the hushed reverence in a sacred space; the tanka, in its elegance and restraint, can capture that same essence. It demands precision, a careful selection of words to convey the weight of profound experiences.

Consider the imagery: a single blossoming lotus flower emerging from murky water, representing spiritual awakening. Or the solitary mountain peak piercing the clouds, symbolizing the striving for enlightenment. These aren't merely descriptions; they are evocative symbols, imbued with layers of meaning, precisely what the spiritual quest is all about. The very act of crafting such imagery within the confines of the tanka becomes a form of meditation, a journey inward.

Many great poets have used the tanka to explore themes of faith, doubt, and the search for meaning. Their work often conveys a sense of awe before the natural world, seeing in its cycles a reflection of the human spiritual journey. Think of the changing seasons, the cycle of life and death—all potent metaphors that can be brilliantly rendered in the concise structure of a tanka, a miniature reflection of the vast cosmos. The power of the tanka lies not just in its aesthetic beauty, but in its ability to speak to the deepest parts of the human soul.

To write effectively about spiritual quests within the tanka form requires introspection. You must delve into your own experiences, wrestling with your beliefs, your doubts, your hopes. This process, while demanding, can be deeply rewarding. It is through honest self-reflection that you will discover the language to express your personal spiritual journey in a way that resonates with your reader. Don't shy away from exploring the darkness alongside the light, the uncertainty along with the certainty. These contrasts often provide the most compelling narratives.

Finding the right words is critical. Unlike free verse, the constraints of the tanka force you to be precise. Every syllable, every word, carries weight. Avoid clichés and generalities. Instead, seek fresh and unexpected imagery to capture the unique nuances of your experience. Consider using sensory details to enhance the reader's connection to the poem. What sounds did you hear during your most profound spiritual moments? What scents, tastes, or textures are associated with those experiences? Bringing these senses to the forefront intensifies the experience for your reader.

A well-crafted tanka on a spiritual theme can be profoundly moving. It is not enough to simply describe the quest; you must convey the emotion behind it—the yearning, the struggle, the eventual peace or understanding. This requires a delicate balance of imagery, rhythm, and tone. A rushed or clumsy tanka will fail to resonate. The beauty and power of the tanka lie in its ability to convey a wealth of meaning through economy of words. The process of crafting such a poem, therefore, is in itself a spiritual practice.

Consider the rhythm and flow of your poem. The structure itself can contribute to the spiritual feeling you aim for. A slower, more deliberate rhythm can convey a sense of contemplation; a faster, more energetic rhythm might express excitement or anticipation. Experiment with different rhythms until you find one that suits your subject matter and your emotional intent. The placement of line breaks is important too, determining the pacing and emphasis of the poem. These subtle adjustments can make all the difference in the final impact of your work.

Remember, your spiritual quest is personal and unique. Don't try to emulate others. Strive for authenticity. Your voice is what will make your tanka truly meaningful. Embrace your individuality, your imperfections, your doubts; these are all essential aspects of the spiritual journey. The process of writing itself is a form of self-discovery. Through careful reflection and honest expression, you can transform your personal experience into a poem that can resonate deeply with others who have traversed a similar path. Let your words echo the resonance of your soul's journey. The tanka, in its smallness, can hold the immensity of the human spiritual quest.

3 Chapter 3: Mastering Technique

Word choice is paramount in tanka. Each syllable carries weight; precision is key. Avoid clichés and generic language. Strive for vivid, concrete imagery that evokes a strong sensory response. Consider the connotations of words, their emotional resonance, and their ability to paint a picture in the reader's mind. For example, instead of "sad," consider "twilight weeping," a far more evocative image. The difference between "happy" and "sun-drenched laughter" is immense. Experiment with synonyms, exploring their subtle nuances to find the perfect fit for your poem's emotional landscape. Remember, even the smallest word choice can dramatically alter the poem's impact. Selecting words carefully is the cornerstone of effective tanka writing, enhancing the overall impact and creating a lasting impression on the reader.

Line breaks are more than just visual divisions; they're powerful tools for controlling the poem's rhythm and pacing. They dictate the reader's breath, influencing the emotional trajectory. A short line can create a sense of urgency or brevity, while a longer line can allow for a more expansive, flowing feeling. Experiment with different line placements to find the most effective way to convey your intended emotion. Notice how the pause created by the line break can affect the meaning. Consider, for instance, the difference in feeling between a line ending with a verb versus a noun. The strategic use of the line break enhances the impact of your imagery and dictates the overall emotional effect of your tanka.

Rhythm and flow are intimately linked to line breaks and word choice. The skillful interplay of these elements creates a musicality that enhances the emotional resonance of the tanka. Aim for a natural rhythm that feels comfortable to read aloud. This often involves a balance of long and short lines, and a variety of syllable stresses. Practice reading your work aloud, listening for any jarring or unnatural pauses. Adjust your line breaks and word choices until the rhythm feels smooth and effortless, enhancing the poem's appeal and readability. The successful blend of rhythmic elements and line placement makes all the difference in the impact of your tanka.

Creating atmosphere is crucial. Use sensory details—sight, sound, smell, taste, touch—to immerse the reader in the poem's world. Vivid descriptions allow the reader to experience the moment alongside the poet. Consider the setting, the time of day, the weather, and the overall mood. Remember the power of evocative imagery—a single well-chosen detail can conjure a whole atmosphere. If you're writing about loss, consider the specific sounds or images associated with grief to convey it effectively and make the tanka deeply moving. The evocative quality of your words transforms the tanka into an experience for your reader.

Revising your work is an essential stage in the crafting process. Don't be afraid to cut words and lines; even seemingly perfect phrases might hinder the poem's overall flow. Read your tanka aloud several times, listening for any awkward phrasing or repetitive imagery. Compare different versions, weighing the impact of minor changes. Be critical; the goal is to maximize impact and emotional resonance, crafting a succinct and emotionally compelling poem. Consider getting feedback from trusted readers, always remembering the aim is to create the most impactful and concise version of your work. Revision is not just about polishing; it's about refining and honing your poem to its most potent form.

3.1   Word Choice

Precision in word choice is paramount in tanka. Each syllable carries weight; each word, a carefully considered brushstroke on the canvas of emotion. Avoid vague language. Instead, opt for strong verbs and concrete nouns that paint vivid pictures in the reader's mind. Think of the subtle difference between "sad" and "desolate," "happy" and "exuberant." The more specific your language, the more deeply your readers will connect with your poem's emotional core. The impact of your carefully chosen words will resonate profoundly.

Consider the power of sensory details. Instead of simply stating "a beautiful day," try "sun-drenched fields whispering secrets to the breeze," engaging multiple senses to create a more immersive and memorable experience. This approach transforms simple observation into evocative imagery. Remember, you want your reader not only to read your words but to feel them.

The selection of verbs demands equal care. Weak verbs like "is" or "was" often lack the dynamism required in tanka. Strong verbs, on the other hand, inject vitality and precision into your writing. "The sun blazed," for instance, is far more impactful than "The sun was shining." This heightened intensity enhances the overall emotional effect. Always seek the most potent verb to convey the feeling you intend to elicit.

Figurative language, used judiciously, can enhance the emotional depth of your tanka. Metaphors, similes, and personification can add layers of meaning and create unexpected connections between seemingly disparate elements. However, avoid overusing figurative language; subtle hints are often more effective than overt declarations. Simplicity and clarity remain key elements.

Synonyms can sometimes be your friend, sometimes your foe. While synonyms provide alternatives, always choose the word that most accurately reflects the nuance of emotion you wish to express. A single word can dramatically alter the impact of your tanka. Carefully consider the connotations of your word choices; the implied meaning is as important as the explicit meaning.

Consider the rhythm and sound of your words. Alliteration, assonance, and consonance can create a pleasing musicality, enhancing the poem's overall effect. This is not to suggest forcing these literary devices into your tanka; their use must remain natural and organic, complementing the poem's emotional core. The rhythm created through careful selection of words will enhance the aesthetic appeal of your work.

Beyond individual words, consider the interplay between words within a line and across the poem's five lines. The arrangement of words affects the pace, flow, and emotional impact. Experiment with different word orders to find the most effective arrangement to amplify the poem's emotional impact. This process will allow for the perfect arrangement of words to portray the emotions you want to express through your tanka.

Remember, word choice is not a mere technical exercise; it is an art form in itself. Every word contributes to the overall impact of your tanka, shaping its emotional landscape and resonance. Mastering this skill involves continuous learning, experimentation, and a deep sensitivity to language's power and emotional capabilities. This is essential for creating moving and poignant works of art. The more you understand the power of words, the more effective your tanka will be. Through careful consideration of these elements, you can craft tankas that resonate with emotional depth and authenticity. The power of your language will allow you to communicate the deepest aspects of the human experience. A well-chosen word can be the difference between a good tanka and a truly exceptional one. Your word choices are the tools of your poetic craft.

Embrace the challenge of finding the perfect words. Your mastery of language will be reflected in the emotional depth of your work, creating a powerful connection between your poem and the reader. Your dedication to precise word choice will become the hallmark of your style, setting your writing apart. The choice of each single word contributes to the overall effect. This is the essence of this art.

3.2   Line Breaks

Line breaks in tanka aren't merely visual cues; they're powerful tools shaping the poem's rhythm, pacing, and emotional impact. Think of them as breaths within the poem, carefully placed to guide the reader's experience. A well-placed break can amplify a moment of tension, create a subtle pause for reflection, or even shift the poem's emotional direction entirely. Mastering this subtle art elevates your tanka from a simple five-line structure to a dynamic, emotionally resonant piece.

Consider the feeling of a long, unbroken line. It often suggests a continuous flow, perhaps a narrative unfolding without interruption. Conversely, a series of short, sharp lines creates a sense of fragmentation, possibly reflecting a broken heart or a fragmented memory. The strategic use of enjambment—the continuation of a sentence or phrase without a pause beyond the line break—adds another layer of complexity. Enjambment can build suspense, create a feeling of unexpectedness, or even disrupt the reader's expectations.

For instance, imagine a tanka about a sunset. A single, long line describing the fiery spectacle could convey a sense of overwhelming beauty. However, breaking that same description into shorter lines, each focusing on a specific detail – the crimson hues, the fading light, the silhouette of distant trees – could evoke a more contemplative, introspective mood. The effect is subtle yet significant. The reader's engagement shifts from simply appreciating the scene to actively participating in its unfolding. This is the power of deliberate line breaks.

Let's explore how line breaks affect meaning. Consider a tanka describing a quiet moment of reflection. Placing the break after the third line, before a pivotal image, emphasizes the transition. This technique allows the reader to fully absorb the preceding lines before encountering the image that brings the poem's central message into focus, creating a significant emotional impact. In contrast, shorter lines emphasizing individual words or phrases can highlight their importance, calling attention to particular sensory details or emotional nuances.

Experiment with different line breaks within the same tanka to understand their impact. Start with a version that uses no enjambment, then try another with different placements. Read each version aloud. Pay attention to how the rhythm changes and how the various line breaks affect the feeling evoked. You might discover that a seemingly minor shift in lineation drastically alters the emotional resonance of your poem. This process of experimentation is crucial.

Remember that the goal isn't to follow rigid rules but to explore the possibilities. There are no right or wrong answers when it comes to line breaks. The best placement often depends on the poem's overall meaning and your intention for the reader's experience. The subtle art of line breaks allows for nuance and variation, inviting the reader to actively participate in the unfolding of your poem.

This experimentation becomes even more significant when you consider the tanka's brevity. Each line carries significant weight, and the strategic placement of line breaks maximizes that weight. Every break shapes how the reader perceives the individual phrases and the relationships between them. Through careful observation and mindful practice, you will master this skill, developing an intuitive understanding of how line breaks amplify the emotional power of your tanka.

Ultimately, the effective use of line breaks is a matter of sensitivity and a keen understanding of rhythm. By paying close attention to the subtle shifts in emphasis and pacing created by various line breaks, you can elevate your tanka from a simple expression of feeling to a powerful and emotionally compelling work of art. So, experiment, revise, and most importantly, listen to the rhythm of your words as you refine your use of the line break. Your tanka will gain depth through the precise placements, enriching both the writing process and the poem itself.

3.3   Rhythm & Flow

The essence of a successful tanka lies not just in adhering to the five-line structure, but in cultivating a natural rhythm and flow. Think of it as a carefully orchestrated dance, each line a measured step, leading the reader seamlessly through the poem's emotional landscape. A jerky, disjointed rhythm will disrupt this flow, leaving the reader feeling lost and unfulfilled. Conversely, a well-crafted tanka feels effortless, its meaning unfolding naturally and gracefully.

Achieving this rhythmic grace often involves subtle manipulations of word choice and line breaks. Experiment with strong verbs and evocative nouns. Short, impactful words can create a sense of urgency or intimacy, while longer, more descriptive words can evoke a sense of spaciousness or grandeur. The interplay of these word choices, carefully considered, is crucial in establishing the poem's rhythmic pulse. Don't underestimate the power of a single, perfectly chosen word to shift the entire tone and rhythm of your tanka.

Line breaks, too, are not arbitrary. They're tools to shape the pace and emphasis of your poem. A shorter line can create a sense of breathlessness, perhaps reflecting a sudden emotion or fleeting moment. A longer line might suggest a more expansive feeling, a leisurely unfolding of thought or imagery. Consider how the pauses created by these breaks affect the overall rhythm. Try different combinations until you find the arrangement that best captures the feeling of your poem. Don't be afraid to experiment. The most beautiful rhythms often emerge from unexpected places.

Remember, the rhythm of a tanka is not merely a technical matter; it's deeply connected to the emotion you wish to convey. A melancholic tanka might benefit from a slower, more deliberate rhythm, reflecting the weight of the feeling. In contrast, a celebratory tanka might have a more lively, buoyant rhythm, mirroring the joy and excitement. Pay close attention to the feeling you aim to create; it will guide you in shaping the rhythm of your words. Always read your tanka aloud. This simple act can reveal surprising rhythms and imbalances you may not have noticed when reading silently.

Beyond individual lines, consider the overall flow between them. The transition from one line to the next should be smooth and natural, avoiding jarring shifts in tone or subject. This requires careful consideration of how your images, ideas, and emotions connect. Use transitions subtly, relying on word associations and implied connections rather than abrupt changes. The goal is to create a seamless journey for the reader, allowing them to become fully immersed in your poem's emotional world. A skillful tanka reads like a single continuous thought, its elements woven together in a cohesive and satisfying whole.

Developing a strong sense of rhythm and flow in your tankas takes practice. It's a process of refining your ear and developing your sensitivity to the subtle nuances of language. Start by reading many tankas, paying attention to the rhythm and flow of each. Observe how accomplished poets use word choice and line breaks to create different effects. Analyze their techniques, and try incorporating them into your own writing. Imitation is a valuable learning tool, but strive to eventually develop your own unique style and voice.

Don't be discouraged if your initial attempts feel clumsy or uneven. The development of skill in tanka writing, as in any art form, requires time, patience, and persistent effort. Embrace experimentation. Try writing tankas on different themes and in different styles. Don't be afraid to break the rules occasionally, to push the boundaries of the form. Through persistent experimentation and self-reflection, you will gradually develop a keen sense of rhythm and flow, enabling you to craft tankas that resonate deeply with your readers. The reward for this dedication is the ability to express profound emotions with concise and elegant grace, a mastery only achieved through understanding and applying the principles of rhythm and flow. The journey itself, with its challenges and triumphs, is an integral part of the creative process. So, continue writing, continue learning, and continue refining your craft until your words flow effortlessly onto the page, carrying your emotions with graceful precision. Your unique voice will emerge, ready to share its story with the world.

3.4   Creating Atmosphere

The air hangs heavy, thick with the scent of petrichor. Rain, recently fallen, clings to the thirsty earth, a subtle sheen on the newly-washed leaves. This is the foundation, the raw material of atmosphere in your tanka. Don't just describe the scene; feel it. Imagine the coolness on your skin, the dampness underfoot, the quiet hum of the world after a storm. Let this sensory experience inform your word choice, guiding you towards evocative language that paints a vivid picture for your reader. Remember, atmosphere isn't merely background; it's a character in its own right, shaping the mood and emotion of your poem. Consider the impact of a single, perfectly chosen word – "murmur," for instance, instead of "sound," or "shimmering" in place of "shiny."

Your choice of imagery is paramount. Think beyond mere description. Use metaphors and similes to create unexpected connections, painting vivid pictures that resonate deeply. Instead of stating that the setting sun is beautiful, compare its hues to a spilled jewel box, or a dying ember's soft glow. These comparisons elevate the commonplace, transforming the ordinary into something extraordinary. This is where your skill in creating atmosphere truly shines; through careful selection, you craft a mood, drawing the reader into the heart of your poem's emotion. The goal is to transport the reader not just to a place, but to a feeling.

Let's explore sound. The rhythm and flow of your tanka are as crucial as the imagery. Consider the sounds of the words themselves – harsh consonants, soft vowels. Do these sounds mirror the atmosphere you're trying to create? A poem about a bustling marketplace might utilize sharp, staccato sounds, whereas one centered on a quiet forest might embrace softer, more flowing sounds. Experiment with assonance and consonance, the repetition of vowel and consonant sounds respectively, to enhance the musicality and create a sense of harmony or dissonance, depending on your desired effect. Remember, the music of the language enhances the overall mood.

Line breaks are another powerful tool in your arsenal. The way you divide your lines can dramatically alter the pacing and emphasis of your tanka. A short line creates a pause, drawing attention to the following words. A longer line might build suspense or emphasize a particular image. Consider where you place line breaks carefully, strategically crafting the rhythm and flow to amplify the poem's atmosphere. Don't think of line breaks as merely formatting; they're tools for sculpting the emotional arc of your poem. A well-placed line break can create a breathtaking shift in perspective.

Now, let's consider the broader context. Think about the overall feeling you want to evoke – serenity, tension, joy, sorrow? The atmosphere you build should be in harmony with the poem's theme and emotional core. A tanka about grief might employ muted colours and melancholic imagery, while one celebrating spring might use vibrant language and uplifting imagery. Ensure that every element, from word choice to line breaks, contributes to this carefully crafted mood. The atmosphere shouldn't feel arbitrary; it needs to be organic, stemming directly from the poem's heart. The atmosphere is not merely a backdrop; it's the emotional canvas upon which your poem is painted.

Finally, revision is essential. Once you've drafted your tanka, revisit it with a critical eye. Does the atmosphere you've created align with the poem's central theme? Are there any jarring notes that disrupt the flow? Are your word choices precise and evocative enough? The process of refining your work is where you hone your craft, transforming a good tanka into a truly exceptional one. Remember, the most powerful atmospheres are subtle yet pervasive, lingering in the reader's mind long after they've finished reading your words. This final step is the key to unlocking the true power of atmosphere in your tanka.

3.5   Revising Your Work

Reworking your tanka isn't about erasing imperfections; it's about sculpting the raw material into something sharper, more resonant. Think of it as a delicate dance between your initial vision and the poem's final form. Each revision offers a chance to refine the emotional impact, to clarify the image, and to strengthen the connection between words. It's a crucial step, often overlooked, but the one that truly elevates a good tanka into something extraordinary.

Consider the power of individual words. Did you choose the most precise verbs and nouns? Are there any unnecessary adjectives or adverbs diluting the poem's impact? Removing extraneous words is often more effective than adding. Experiment with synonyms. Sometimes a seemingly small change can drastically shift the poem's mood or meaning. A single word, perfectly chosen, can illuminate the entire piece.

Line breaks are more than just visual punctuation; they shape the rhythm and pace of your tanka. Experiment with different configurations. Where does a natural pause occur? Does shifting a line break alter the emphasis on a specific image or emotion? Play with the music of your language; the cadence of a well-crafted line contributes significantly to the overall experience. Consider your reader; the flow of the tanka should guide them seamlessly.

Revisit the kigo—that essential seasonal word. Does it truly resonate with the overall feeling of the poem? Does it add layers of meaning, or is it simply present for the sake of fulfilling a structural requirement? Sometimes even a subtle adjustment to the kigo can unlock a new depth of meaning, linking the poem's emotional core to the natural world. Remember the powerful synergy of word and image.

The imagery in your tanka is your storytelling tool. Are your images vivid and evocative? Can the reader easily visualize what you're describing? Look for areas where your descriptions could become more precise, more sensory. Instead of saying "a cold day," could you convey the feeling more vividly, perhaps with "frost clinging to withered leaves"? Such detailed sensory language allows the reader to fully immerse themselves in your poem's world.

Now, let's address the overall structure. Does each line serve a purpose? Do they build upon each other to create a coherent and emotionally satisfying whole? Consider the emotional arc of the tanka. Does it start subtly, building to a powerful conclusion or perhaps utilizing a different structure? Analyze the way your lines flow; sometimes rearranging can greatly improve the poem's effectiveness. Try reading it aloud to uncover areas of awkwardness or unevenness.

Once you've made significant revisions, step away from your work for a day or two. Returning with fresh eyes allows you to spot lingering weaknesses you might have missed previously. Consider sharing your work with a trusted peer or joining a writing group for constructive feedback. Objective opinions can offer invaluable insights and illuminate areas you might not have even considered.

Revision is not simply about correcting errors; it's about a continuous process of refinement and growth. Embrace the iterative nature of writing, view every revision as an opportunity for deepening the emotional resonance of your tanka. Each time you rework, you're not just editing; you're sculpting, honing your craft, bringing your initial vision into increasingly sharper focus, and transforming a simple poem into something truly profound. The process is not just about perfecting the form, but about uncovering the heart of your work, allowing its emotional truth to shine through. Remember that even seasoned poets continuously refine their works; this chapter simply highlights the vital role revision plays in their ongoing development.

4 Chapter 4: Structure & Meaning

Developing a tanka isn't simply about fitting syllables into a pre-defined mold; it's about weaving a tapestry of meaning. Think of the structure as a framework, a guide for your thoughts, not a cage to restrict them. Each line, with its specific syllable count, contributes to the poem's rhythm and the overall impact. The shorter lines, for example, can create a sense of urgency or breathlessness, while the longer lines can evoke a feeling of expansiveness or contemplation. The subtle shifts in length, if carefully considered, become powerful tools in your poetic arsenal.

Start with a core idea, a single image, or a powerful emotion. Don't worry about perfection at this stage; let your thoughts flow freely. Perhaps a fleeting memory sparked an emotional response, a vibrant scene caught your eye, or an abstract concept has ignited your imagination. Jot down everything, however fragmented or incomplete it may seem. Freewriting exercises can be particularly helpful at this point. Don't censor yourself; the goal is to uncover the raw material, the essence of what you want to convey.

Once you have a collection of thoughts and ideas, begin to arrange them, shaping your core concept into a coherent narrative. This is where the tanka's structure becomes critical. Consider how your chosen images and details relate to one another, and how they contribute to the overall impact you aim to create. Experiment with different arrangements, testing how each line interacts with its neighbors. Perhaps you find that moving a line changes the emphasis, shifting the poem's mood from joy to sorrow or from excitement to serenity. This is the beautiful dance of structure and meaning.

Finding your unique voice in tanka is a journey of self-discovery. It's about developing a style that is authentic to you, one that reflects your individual perspective and emotional landscape. This isn't about mimicking the styles of others; it's about learning from them, finding inspiration, and then creating something entirely your own. Experiment with different techniques, explore unconventional imagery, and don't be afraid to push boundaries. Remember, the most compelling tankas are often those that feel both deeply personal and universally relatable.

Don't underestimate the power of revision. Once you've crafted a complete tanka, step back and assess your work with a fresh perspective. Are there words or phrases that could be more evocative? Is the rhythm satisfying? Does the structure effectively convey your meaning? Consider consulting with other writers for feedback – a new perspective can often illuminate aspects of your work that you haven't noticed yourself. The process of revision is essential to refining your craft and honing your unique poetic voice. Remember that the goal is not just to write a tanka that meets the formal requirements, but to craft a poem that resonates deeply with the reader, leaving a lasting impression. The interplay between careful structure and well-chosen words is what elevates a good tanka into a truly memorable one. The structure, while seemingly simple, is the vehicle for your meaning; use it wisely, and you'll find that the constraints of the form become a source of creative freedom. Experiment, revise, and let your own voice emerge, and through this process, your journey as a tanka poet will unfold, bringing forth pieces that are uniquely yours and resonate with the depths of human experience.

4.1 Developing Ideas

Begin with a single, potent image. A flickering candle flame, perhaps, reflecting in a rain-streaked windowpane. Let that image become the seed of your tanka. Don't force it; let the image settle, grow roots in your mind. Consider the emotions it evokes: loneliness, peace, anticipation? These feelings, however subtle, are the key to unlocking the poem's potential. The initial inspiration, however fleeting, needs nurturing, careful consideration, and attention to detail. Develop it by exploring its nuances. What is the context? What story does this image hint at? What is not said adds as much weight as what you express.

Now, consider the context surrounding that image. Is it a cold winter night, evoking a sense of isolation? Or is it a quiet moment during a summer storm, a time of reflection and introspection? Perhaps the image is more abstract – a memory, a feeling. Regardless, the key is to build a narrative arc, however small, within your five lines. The tanka isn't just a collection of pretty words; it's a miniature world, complete with its own emotional landscape. Develop this microcosm with precision. A thoughtful approach to the smallest details is crucial. This meticulous process leads to a more impactful experience.

Your tanka will benefit from a clear focus. Avoid trying to cram too many ideas into this compact form. Resist the urge to tell a complete story. Instead, focus on a single, powerful moment, a specific emotion, a carefully observed detail. The beauty of the tanka lies in its ability to convey immense depth through economy of expression. This requires discipline, the ability to choose the most effective words. Editing can lead to the most beautiful results, and revision is critical in refining the piece.

Consider the rhythm and flow of your words. The tanka's structure—five lines with a specific syllable count—naturally lends itself to a certain musicality. Experiment with word placement; a carefully chosen line break can dramatically alter the poem's effect. Try different word options; each one alters the tone and atmosphere. Consider the sounds the words make and how they flow together. A skillful arrangement of words, in this short format, can lead to a sublime piece of art.

Don't be afraid to experiment. Try writing several variations of your initial idea, playing with different word choices, images, and perspectives. Each attempt might reveal a new facet of the idea, bringing you closer to the heart of your poem. The essence of good writing comes from careful consideration, reflection and testing out various options. The final form shouldn't feel forced; it should feel natural, inevitable.

As you develop your idea, remember the importance of "kigo," seasonal words. These words act as anchors, grounding your poem in the natural world. The subtle shift in seasons, the changing light, the subtle scents—these elements can add depth and resonance to your work. If your poem is about a candle flame, for example, consider the season. Is it the gentle warmth of a summer evening, the desperate need for light against the long winter night, or something else? Each season offers its own unique emotional palette, enriching your piece.

Once you have a draft, step away from it for a while. Return with fresh eyes, and read your tanka aloud. Does it sound right? Does it capture the emotion you intended? Be honest in your self-assessment. If not, don't hesitate to revise; the final product should be a refined form of your initial idea. Remember, the tanka is a journey of refinement. Each word, each image, should contribute to the overall effect.

Finally, trust your intuition. The best tankas often arise from a place of genuine emotion, a deep personal connection with the subject matter. Your unique perspective, your individual voice, is what will make your tanka truly sing. Let your personal feelings be the guide, and allow your individual voice to shine through. This authentic expression will resonate with readers, making your work memorable and powerful. Don't be afraid to be vulnerable; authentic feelings will always produce the best results.

4.2 Finding Your Voice

Your voice, in tanka, isn't about mimicking others; it's about finding the unique way you see the world, the emotions that resonate uniquely within you. It's not about perfection, but about honesty. Consider this: your experiences, your perspectives, are unlike anyone else's. Those very things—the things that make you, you—form the bedrock of your unique poetic voice. Perhaps you've loved deeply, experienced loss profoundly, or felt the awe-inspiring vastness of nature. These powerful emotions aren't just fodder for tanka; they're the fuel. Draw strength from these intense, personal experiences. Don't shy away from the rawness of your emotions; embrace them. They are the wellspring of authentic expression, forming the foundation of your individual style within the tanka form. Your experiences are uniquely yours, your perspective unparalleled. Let that truth shine through.

Experiment. Try writing about different things, exploring various styles.

Don't be afraid to break the rules, to bend the form, to push boundaries. See what happens when you deliberately use unusual imagery or unexpected juxtapositions. Perhaps try different sentence structures or unusual word choices. The important thing is to discover what feels right for you. Remember, the tanka's structure is a guide, not a cage.

Avoid clichés. They might seem easy, but they lack originality. Instead, strive for precision. Choose your words meticulously; each syllable should carry weight, resonate with emotion, paint a picture. Focus on creating vivid imagery that pulls the reader into your world. Consider the emotional weight of each carefully chosen word, allowing your meaning to fully develop organically.

Read widely. Immerse yourself in the works of established tanka poets. Pay close attention to their technique, their style, their use of language. But don't just imitate; analyze. Identify what resonates with you, what moves you, what inspires you. Discover what aspects of their style align with your own creative vision. This analytical approach will hone your skills. Understand why their work is successful. Analyze this to better inform your own creative approach.

Seek feedback, but trust your instincts. Sharing your work with others can provide valuable insights, helping you identify areas for improvement. However, ultimately, the voice you use in your tanka must be authentically yours. Don't let external opinions dilute your personal expression, ensuring the final outcome reflects your unique viewpoint. The final poem should be one you're proud to own.

Remember that your voice is not static; it evolves over time. As you write more, as you gain experience, your style will mature, your perspective will deepen. Embrace this journey of self-discovery. Finding your voice in tanka is an ongoing process, a continuous exploration of self and expression. Each tanka becomes a step in understanding the nuances of your unique artistic voice. This ongoing process forms the very heart of your tanka journey.

Don't be discouraged by setbacks. Writing is a craft, and like any craft, it takes time and practice to master. There will be times when you feel frustrated, when your words don't seem to capture what you want to express. Persistence is crucial. Keep writing, keep experimenting, keep pushing yourself. The more you practice, the stronger your voice will become, allowing for more nuanced and profound expressions through your tanka. Ultimately, your voice in tanka is about authenticity. It's about expressing your unique perspective, your unique emotions, in a concise and powerful way. It's about connecting with your inner self and sharing that connection with the world. And it's a journey, one that will continue to unfold as you develop your skills and explore your personal experiences, continually refining your craft and the beauty of your voice. That's what makes this journey of crafting tanka so exceptionally compelling and worthwhile. Embrace the process, and let your unique voice shine through.

5 Chapter 5: Inspiration & Practice

Daily writing is key. Think of it as a muscle; the more you use it, the stronger it becomes. Start small. Five minutes a day is better than nothing. Set a timer, find a quiet space, and just write. Don't worry about perfection; just let the words flow. Focus on capturing a feeling, an image, a fleeting thought. You might be surprised by what emerges. Remember those feelings of awe you had when you saw the sunset? Or that moment of intense joy from a childhood memory? Those feelings are raw materials, gold for your tanka. Don't be afraid to revisit these memories and emotions, they are part of your unique experience that will make your poems original and meaningful.

Reading widely is equally vital. Immerse yourself in the work of established tanka poets. Explore different styles, themes, and techniques. Pay attention to their word choices, their use of imagery, and the overall emotional impact of their poems. This is not about imitation; it's about learning from masters and understanding the full potential of the form. What made this poet choose these specific words? How did they craft their rhythm and flow to convey that specific emotion? It's not just about reading, but actively analyzing. Take your favourite tanka. Try to rewrite it, then analyze the result and find the things you liked and disliked about it. This method will help you develop a sharper eye and a better understanding of what makes a tanka resonate.

Seeking feedback is crucial. Share your work with trusted friends, fellow writers, or even online communities dedicated to poetry. Constructive criticism can help you identify weaknesses in your work and refine your craft. Don't be afraid of criticism; instead, view it as an opportunity for growth. Remember, not everyone will appreciate your work, and that is perfectly fine. The important thing is to find those who can offer insightful and supportive feedback. Join online writing groups and workshops – sharing your work allows you to receive feedback from other writers, and to learn from their creative journey too. A community of writers can offer unique perspectives and constructive criticism. Don't be afraid to share your work and be open to suggestions, it can be an enriching and transformative experience.

It's not enough to just write; you must actively engage with the process. Experiment with different forms and styles. Don't be afraid to break the rules (once you understand them). Let your emotions guide you; let your voice shine through. The tanka is a small form, but it's capable of expressing a vast range of human experiences. The more you practice, the more adept you will become at conveying those experiences with precision and power. Practice, practice, practice! And never stop learning, always seek to improve and grow. You will find your own unique voice and style, a unique way of expressing your feelings and emotions in five lines.

Remember the power of observation. The world is full of inspiration – in nature, in relationships, in everyday moments. Pay attention to the details. Notice the way the light catches the leaves, the sound of rain on a tin roof, the subtle shift in someone's expression. These observations are the seeds of your tanka. Capture these moments, these seemingly minor details, and transform them into something beautiful and meaningful. These little details are often where the powerful emotions reside. And don't underestimate the power of stillness and reflection. Sometimes, the most profound insights come from quiet moments of contemplation. Allow yourself time to process your experiences and let your emotions settle before you begin writing. Use this time for reflection, to discover the true core of the emotion you want to express.

5.1 Daily Writing

The key to unlocking your potential as a tanka writer lies in consistent practice. Think of it like any other craft—a musician's daily scales, a painter's dedicated sketching, a sculptor's careful chiseling. Daily writing isn't about producing masterpieces every time; it's about building the muscles of your poetic mind, strengthening your ability to observe, to distill, to express. Set aside even just fifteen minutes each day, a small commitment that yields significant returns over time. You might be surprised at the unexpected insights and poetic sparks that surface in those dedicated moments.

Consistency is paramount. Don't let a missed day snowball into a week, then a month, of inaction. Life inevitably throws curveballs, but make a conscious effort to re-engage as soon as possible. If you miss a day, don't beat yourself up about it. Simply pick up your pen or open your document and start again. The most important thing is to maintain the momentum, that steady rhythm of creative engagement.

Choose a time of day that works best for you. Are you a morning person, finding clarity before the day's demands? Or do you find your creative juices flowing in the quiet stillness of the evening? Find your peak creative time, and make it your daily ritual. This consistency will train your brain to expect and anticipate these moments of artistic creation, and make your tanka journey more fulfilling.

Experiment with different prompts. Use a single image, a memory, a overheard conversation, a snippet of a song – anything that sparks your imagination. The goal isn't necessarily a perfect tanka; instead, it's to practice the art of observation and transformation, to see the world through a tanka-shaped lens, to hone the skill of capturing essence in the form. Keep a notebook handy to jot down ideas that strike you throughout the day, and then dive into writing during your dedicated time.

Don't be afraid to write badly. Early attempts often feel awkward or clumsy. This is perfectly normal. Embrace the imperfections; they're part of the learning process. See each tanka as a stepping stone, a bridge to a more refined expression. The act of writing itself is more important than achieving immediate perfection. Keep refining your process and you'll see improvement.

Read widely. Immerse yourself in the work of established tanka poets. Pay attention to their word choices, their imagery, their use of kigo (seasonal words). Analyze how they create atmosphere, rhythm, and emotional depth within the strictures of the form. Inspiration is often found in the work of others; use it as fuel for your creative fire. Remember what you read and how it inspires you.

Seek feedback, but carefully consider the source. Share your work with trusted readers—friends, writing group members, or mentors—who can offer constructive criticism. Be discerning in your choice of critics, however; not all feedback is equally valuable. Look for insightful observations that help you improve your work, rather than vague praise or unhelpful criticism.

Remember that daily writing is a marathon, not a sprint. Progress isn't always linear, and there will be days when you struggle. But consistency is key. Keep showing up, keep writing, keep learning, and you'll steadily improve your skills and discover your unique voice within the concise and emotionally powerful world of tanka. Your dedication will pay off. Trust the process and enjoy the journey.

5.2   Reading Great Tankas

Reading great tankas isn't just about passively absorbing words; it's about actively engaging with the poet's craft, understanding their choices, and feeling the emotional resonance they create. Begin by choosing a collection or anthology featuring established tanka poets. Don't just skim; truly immerse yourself in each poem. Pay attention to the rhythm, the way the syllables fall, and how the pauses between lines affect the overall feel.

Notice how the poet uses kigo, those seasonal words we discussed in Chapter 1. How does the kigo not only contribute to the imagery, but also to the mood and overall message? Does it evoke a specific time of year, a particular feeling connected to that season, or even a broader emotional landscape? Analyze how this careful choice shapes your understanding of the poem's deeper meaning. Consider the interplay between the imagery and the emotional core of the tanka. Are they in harmony, or do they create a sense of contrast or tension? Exploring this interaction is key to appreciating the nuances of masterful tankas.

For example, consider a tanka about a winter scene: the starkness of the landscape might mirror the poet's feelings of isolation or loss, while the enduring strength of a winter tree could symbolize resilience. This is where your understanding of themes, as explored in Chapter 2, becomes invaluable. The best tankas resonate deeply because they speak to universal human experiences, connecting with readers on a visceral level. Therefore, take note of how the poets use imagery and word choice to evoke these feelings.

Next, focus on the structure and meaning, building upon Chapter 4's teachings. How does the poet use the five lines to build suspense, create a sense of movement, or resolve a particular idea? Some poets might lead with a powerful image, then gradually reveal the emotional core, while others might begin with the emotion and use the remaining lines to amplify it with specific imagery. Analyze these choices and consider how they impact the poem's overall effect. Consider the strategic use of line breaks. Where does the poet choose to end a line? Are the breaks natural, enhancing the flow, or are they deliberately jarring, adding a layer of emotional intensity? Don't underestimate the power of repetition. Sometimes, the strategic repetition of a word or phrase can amplify a feeling or create a sense of rhythm. Conversely, the absence of repetition might be just as significant, emphasizing the uniqueness of each line and its individual contribution to the whole. Pay close attention to these subtle details. Remember Chapter 3 and the guidance on word choice and rhythm? Apply that knowledge to your analysis of these chosen tankas. The masters carefully selected every word, utilizing conciseness as their strength. You must do the same when you evaluate their skill.

Now, consider the overall atmosphere the poet created. Is it serene, melancholic, celebratory, or something else entirely? How did they achieve this? By examining the precise word choices, the sensory details, and the overall flow of the poem, you can start to decipher the poet's techniques for building atmosphere. This meticulous analysis will improve your understanding of the tools available to you as a tanka writer. Finally, after completing your analysis, consider writing your own tankas inspired by the work you've studied. Engage in active participation by creating your own responses to these great works, making the process of learning truly transformative and lasting. Seeking feedback, as discussed in Chapter 5, is vital for growth. Your critical reading skills will enhance your creative abilities considerably. Reading great tankas is a crucial step in mastering the art of the tanka.

5.3   Seeking Feedback

Seeking feedback is crucial; it's the bridge between your solitary creation and a wider understanding. Don't shy away from sharing your work, even if it feels vulnerable. Remember, feedback isn't about criticism, it's about growth.

Finding the right people to offer feedback can significantly influence your progress. Seek out individuals who understand tanka, or at least appreciate poetry. Online communities dedicated to poetry offer a wealth of potential feedback providers; browse forums, join groups, and participate in discussions. Don't underestimate the value of in-person workshops; the energy and immediate exchange can be invaluable.

Consider your objectives when choosing who to approach. Do you want someone to focus on the technical aspects, like syllable count and imagery? Or are you hoping for feedback on the emotional impact and overall message? If you're struggling with a specific element, mention it clearly. A focused question provides better results than a broad appeal for feedback.

When you receive feedback, remember this: everyone sees through different lenses. Some may focus on technical elements you've already mastered; others might identify emotional nuances that completely escaped you. Treat all input as a potential insight, even if it doesn't immediately resonate. It is an opportunity to broaden your perspective and learn from other poet's insights.

Remember, feedback isn't a grading exercise. It's not about proving your worth or measuring your talent. It's about refining your craft. Approach each comment with an open mind, questioning, analyzing, and integrating the most useful suggestions. Don't let a single negative comment derail your progress.

Constructive criticism should be specific. Vague comments like "it's good" or "it's not working" are unhelpful. Seek feedback that highlights areas for improvement with suggestions on how to improve them. For example, instead of "The imagery is weak," look for feedback like "The imagery in the second line feels a little distant; consider using more sensory details to bring it to life."

Some feedback may surprise you; don't dismiss it automatically. If multiple people point out a similar issue, even if it's something you didn't initially notice, it's worth considering. It could be a blind spot in your work you can address and improve. Your creative blind spot may be an intriguing feature for another poet.

After receiving feedback, take some time to process it. Don't rush into revisions. Consider each suggestion, reflect on its validity, and decide which ones best support the poem's intended impact. You are the ultimate judge of your work, but other viewpoints provide valuable perspective.

Finally, expressing gratitude for the feedback received, regardless of whether you use all of it, is an act of respect and fosters positive relationships within the poetry community. It keeps the channels of communication open, strengthening collaborative learning and personal growth. It helps you make new friendships. Remember, feedback is a gift, an investment in your growth as a tanka poet.

6 Chapter 6: Sharing Your Work

Sharing your carefully crafted tankas shouldn't feel daunting; it's a celebration of your creative journey. Numerous avenues exist for you to connect with fellow enthusiasts and potential readers, fostering a supportive community and expanding your reach. Consider submitting your work to literary magazines; many specialize in poetry, some even focusing specifically on shorter forms like tanka. Research their submission guidelines meticulously; these often vary widely, impacting the formatting and overall presentation of your poems. Remember that persistence is key—rejections are a common part of the process, but don't let them discourage you from pursuing your goals.

Online platforms offer a different kind of exposure. Websites and social media groups dedicated to poetry provide opportunities to connect with a diverse audience. Engage actively; share your work, offer constructive feedback to others, and participate in discussions. Such platforms allow for immediate feedback and a broader reach than traditional publishing routes, helping you garner both immediate and long-term support. Use these channels to gauge audience response and adapt your style accordingly. Consider establishing your own online presence, perhaps a personal blog or a profile on a platform specifically designed for writers. This allows you to showcase your work consistently, forming a portfolio that demonstrates your creative journey's progress.

Participating in workshops and writing groups provides invaluable support and guidance. The dynamic of a group setting fosters creative exploration;

hearing others read their tankas and receiving feedback helps you to analyze your own work with a fresh perspective. The shared experience of writing provides inspiration and motivation, breaking down the isolation that can sometimes accompany creative endeavors. Actively participate by offering your thoughts and comments. Such involvement is not only beneficial for others but also strengthens your critical skills. Workshops can offer in-person or virtual settings, providing various levels of interaction, depending on your individual preference and circumstances.

Remember, the goal isn't merely to publish; it's to share your unique perspective and connect with others who appreciate your art form. Sharing your work expands its potential audience, increasing the likelihood that your tankas will resonate with readers who deeply appreciate the emotional depth and concise beauty of this poetic form. Don't limit yourself; experiment with different methods, and continue evolving your approach. The act of sharing contributes to a larger artistic conversation, strengthening the community and enriching the collective experience of tanka appreciation. As you share your work, embrace the feedback and the dialogue; these are integral parts of refining your craft and deepening your understanding of the artistry involved in crafting effective tankas.

The journey of a writer involves much more than just creating; it is about sharing your vision with the world. Engaging in these different avenues of sharing and collaboration is crucial to grow and contribute to the evolving art of Tanka. Find the path that suits you and feel confident in sharing your talent and passion. Sharing isn't just about showcasing what you have achieved; it is about building a community, receiving support, and pushing yourself further along your creative pathway. Each opportunity provides unique aspects, allowing you to explore and experience the multifaceted nature of sharing your craft with the world. There is a perfect way for each writer to present their work, and finding the fit between writer and audience is a key element of success.

6.1 Publishing Options

Many avenues exist for sharing your carefully crafted tankas with the world. Submitting your work to literary magazines, both print and online, offers a traditional publishing route. Research magazines specializing in poetry, particularly those featuring shorter forms, to identify suitable targets. Pay close attention to their submission guidelines; following these instructions meticulously shows respect for the editors' time and increases your chances of acceptance. Remember, rejection doesn't signify failure; it's often a stepping stone towards improvement. Persistence pays off.

Online platforms provide a readily accessible alternative. Websites and blogs dedicated to poetry offer opportunities to publish your work and engage with a wider audience. Many platforms cater specifically to tanka, providing a community of like-minded writers and readers. Some platforms allow for direct submission, while others may require joining a group or forum. Explore the different options, paying close attention to each platform's unique guidelines and community standards. This broadens your reach and connects you with other poets.

Self-publishing offers complete control over the presentation and distribution of your work. Creating a collection of your tankas in ebook or print format allows for direct engagement with your audience. Websites like Amazon Kindle Direct Publishing provide user-friendly tools for self-publication, offering options for customizing cover art and formatting. While this route requires more effort in marketing and distribution, it rewards you with complete creative autonomy, allowing for personalization and unique aesthetic choices. This empowers you to directly engage with your audience and share your creative vision without intermediary filters.

Anthologies offer a collaborative pathway to publication. Participating in themed anthologies can expose your work to a wider readership while providing opportunities for networking with other poets. Look for open calls for submissions from established publishers or independent groups. Examine each anthology's theme carefully to ensure your tankas align with the collection's focus. This helps to maintain a coherent collection that resonates with readers. Carefully consider the anthology's reputation and target audience.

Entering poetry contests and competitions provides a chance to gain recognition and potentially win prizes. Many prestigious competitions exist worldwide. Some focus specifically on tanka, while others include it as a category in broader poetry contests. Carefully review each competition's guidelines, including entry fees, deadlines, and eligibility requirements. This process exposes your work to judges and potentially a wider audience, highlighting your talent. Remember that participation itself is a valuable learning experience.

Creating your own website or blog devoted to your poetry provides a personalized space to showcase your tankas. It also allows you to share your creative process, providing insights into your inspirations and techniques. This platform empowers you to establish a unique online presence, engaging directly with your readers. You can also use it to share your writing journey with your audience, adding a personal element to the reading experience. Think of it as your creative hub.

Consider collaborating with visual artists to create collaborative projects. Pairing your tankas with paintings, photographs, or other artwork can create compelling and emotionally resonant pieces. This synergistic approach adds visual dimension to your poetry, broadening the impact and enriching the overall aesthetic experience. Consider approaching local art organizations or artists directly, proposing the collaboration. This interdisciplinary approach can introduce your work to a completely new audience and foster creative growth for both participants. This is a valuable way to diversify your creative work and expand your audience.

Remember, publishing is a multifaceted process, and your approach should reflect your personal preferences and goals. Whether you choose to submit your work to established magazines, embrace the accessibility of online platforms, or explore self-publishing opportunities, each path presents opportunities for growth and connection with a wider community of readers. Enjoy the journey, learn from every experience, and remain passionate about sharing the emotional depth of your carefully crafted tankas. Each experience will contribute to your growth as a writer, expanding your reach and amplifying your voice in the poetic landscape. The key is to experiment, to learn, and to persistently share your unique artistic vision.

6.2 Online Communities

Online communities offer a vibrant landscape for sharing your tanka and engaging with fellow poets. Finding the right community can significantly boost your writing journey, providing invaluable feedback, encouragement, and a sense of belonging. Don't underestimate the power of shared experience; the collective energy of a supportive group can fuel your creative fire and help you overcome creative blocks.

Many online platforms cater specifically to poets. Websites and forums dedicated to poetry often have sections or threads specifically for tanka. These spaces provide a ready-made audience, a place where you can post your work and receive responses. Some platforms may even have dedicated tanka challenges or contests, offering opportunities for exposure and friendly competition. Participation is key to receiving valuable feedback that will help you refine your technique and learn from the experiences of others.

Consider joining social media groups focused on poetry or tanka. Facebook, Instagram, and Twitter all host active communities of writers. Searching for relevant hashtags can lead you to groups with shared interests. Engage actively; participate in discussions, offer constructive criticism to others, and be open to receiving feedback yourself. Remember, building relationships with other poets is a crucial aspect of growth, and these communities provide a platform to make connections that will last far beyond the initial interactions.

While online communities offer significant advantages, approach them with discernment. Not all online interactions are equally constructive. Prioritize groups that emphasize respectful dialogue and constructive criticism. Look for communities that actively moderate content to ensure a positive and encouraging atmosphere. Ignore negativity or any unproductive criticism, and focus on those who offer genuine insight and support that will propel you forward.

Remember, your goal is to learn and grow. Use the online environment as a tool to improve your craft. Don't hesitate to ask questions, express your ideas and seek clarification. Active participation helps hone not only your writing skills, but also your critical thinking and interpersonal communication skills, valuable assets in any creative pursuit. Use this space to explore different perspectives and appreciate the diverse styles and approaches fellow tanka writers bring to the form.

Online workshops and classes can provide more structured learning experiences. Many established poets and instructors offer online workshops through various platforms, some free and some at a price. These structured settings often provide a clear learning path, focusing on specific aspects of tanka writing, and provide the ability to interact more directly with the instructor and fellow students, creating opportunities for tailored feedback and creative collaborations. Consider your learning style and budget when selecting a course, aiming for a program which offers a balance between structured learning and creative exploration.

Exploring different online communities will allow you to discover various perspectives and approaches to tanka writing. You'll encounter poets with different styles, levels of experience, and backgrounds, enriching your understanding of the art form. You may find inspiration in the works of others, or gain a deeper appreciation for the nuances of the tanka through the varied perspectives shared within these diverse groups. Embrace this variety, and use it as a springboard for experimenting with your own writing.

Beyond the technical aspects of the tanka, online communities can offer a much-needed sense of camaraderie and support. The isolation of creative work can be challenging, so building relationships with other poets can offer a powerful antidote to feelings of loneliness. A supportive online community allows you to share your work and receive encouraging feedback without the pressure of in-person interaction. Foster these connections. Remember, a supportive network can be invaluable to any writer. Embrace the connections you build and enjoy the shared journey of crafting beautiful tanka. This shared experience will enrich your understanding and appreciation for the art form and help you grow in ways you may not have anticipated. The power of community shouldn't be underestimated. It's an integral component of your creative development and ongoing success.

6.3   Workshops & Groups

Joining a tanka workshop or writing group offers invaluable benefits beyond solitary practice. The shared experience fosters a supportive environment where you can receive constructive criticism, learn from others, and gain a fresh perspective on your own work. Imagine the energy of a room filled with fellow poets, each bringing their unique voice and experience to the table. This shared space can spark new ideas and inspire you to push your creative boundaries further than you might have on your own.

The dynamic of a workshop setting facilitates a two-way learning process. While receiving feedback on your own poems, you'll simultaneously gain insights into the techniques and approaches used by other writers. This comparative process can be incredibly illuminating, highlighting different ways to achieve similar effects or revealing unexpected approaches you might not have considered. Observing how others navigate the challenges of crafting concise, evocative verse can be just as valuable as receiving direct feedback on your own work.

Beyond the direct feedback, workshops often incorporate exercises and prompts specifically designed to stretch your poetic muscles. These focused activities can help you break through creative blocks, explore new thematic territory, or experiment with different stylistic elements within the tanka form. The structured nature of these exercises can lead to breakthroughs that might otherwise remain elusive. Participating actively in these activities is key to their effectiveness; don't just observe, engage.

Finding the right group is crucial. Consider the size of the group; smaller groups often provide more individualized attention, while larger groups offer a wider range of perspectives and potential collaborations. The experience level of participants should also be a factor. A beginner-friendly group can offer a supportive and non-intimidating environment to start, while a more advanced group might prove challenging but rewarding once you've developed a stronger foundation. Look for groups with a clear focus on tanka, ensuring the instruction and feedback are relevant to your specific needs and goals.

Online communities also present excellent opportunities for connection and feedback, even beyond formal workshops. Many online forums and groups dedicated to poetry offer a space for sharing work, participating in critiques, and engaging in discussions about the craft. These platforms can expand your network of fellow writers, offering a wider perspective and a diverse range of viewpoints on your work. Remember to approach online critique constructively; not all feedback will be positive, but even less-than-stellar comments can identify areas for improvement.

Don't underestimate the power of simply reading and appreciating the work of others. Exposure to different styles, themes, and techniques can be a catalyst for your own artistic growth. Within a workshop or group setting, you're exposed to a variety of writing styles and approaches, which encourages you to experiment and develop your own unique voice. Even if you're not actively participating in critique sessions, simply reading the poems of your peers can provide insights into different perspectives and styles.

Beyond the technical aspects of writing, workshops and groups offer a crucial element: community. The shared passion for tanka can foster a sense of belonging and mutual support, transforming what might initially feel like a solitary pursuit into a collaborative endeavor. This connection with like-minded individuals can sustain your motivation and provide encouragement during times of writer's block or self-doubt.

Remember that a supportive community isn't just about receiving feedback; it's also about giving it. Sharpening your critical eye by offering constructive feedback to others improves your ability to self-edit and understand the nuances of effective tanka writing. Participating in critique sessions, whether online or in person, refines your skills as a reader and writer simultaneously. Engaging fully in this process, offering feedback with sensitivity and constructive intent, enriches the overall learning experience for everyone involved.

The benefits extend beyond the immediate environment of the workshop or online group. The connections you make, the knowledge you gain, and the community you build can have a lasting impact on your artistic journey. These relationships often extend beyond the life of a specific workshop, providing a sustained network of support and inspiration for years to come. Participating in these groups can create lasting bonds with fellow writers, fostering a sense of community that extends beyond the initial course.

Ultimately, engaging with workshops and groups is an investment in your own artistic growth. It's a chance to learn from experienced poets, receive valuable feedback, and connect with a community of like-minded individuals. While solitary practice is essential, the collaborative aspects of workshops and groups are invaluable in refining your skills and fostering your passion for the art of tanka. Embrace this opportunity for growth; it's a journey well worth taking.

7 Chapter 7: The Journey Continues

The beauty of tanka lies not just in its concise structure, but in its capacity for continuous growth. Your journey as a tanka writer is far from over; it's merely the beginning of a lifelong exploration of language, emotion, and self-expression. Consider this chapter a springboard, propelling you toward new heights in your poetic endeavors. Each tanka you craft becomes a stepping stone, leading you to a deeper understanding of both the form and yourself.

Now, having grasped the fundamentals, it's time to delve deeper into the nuances of the art. Experiment with different styles, explore unconventional themes, and challenge yourself to break free from familiar patterns. Don't be afraid to embrace risk; sometimes, the most unexpected choices lead to the most rewarding results. This isn't about perfection; it's about pushing boundaries and refining your craft over time.

Revisit your older work. You'll be surprised at how your perspective has shifted, how your skills have sharpened. Identify the strengths and weaknesses in your early attempts. Use this as a foundation for improvement, recognizing the patterns of your strengths and addressing areas that need attention. The journey isn't linear, it's iterative. There will be moments of frustration, but don't let them discourage you. Instead, allow them to inform your development.

Seek out feedback, but remember to filter it through your own artistic vision. Not every critique will resonate with you, and that's perfectly fine. Trust your instincts, your own emotional connection to the words on the page. The most valuable feedback often comes not from external sources, but from your own heightened awareness as you revisit your writing. This self-assessment is crucial in refining your work.

Beyond the technical aspects, consider the tanka's ability to sharpen your observation skills. Pay closer attention to the world around you—the subtle shifts in light, the nuances of human interaction, the whispering wind. This keen attention to detail will not only enhance your tankas but also enrich your daily life. It fosters a different level of awareness, leading to a more profound understanding of your surroundings and of yourself.

The skills you've acquired through writing tanka are transferable to other forms of creative expression. The precision of language, the ability to evoke emotion through concise imagery—these are valuable assets in any artistic endeavor. You might find yourself drawn to haiku, senryu, or even longer forms of poetry. Perhaps you'll explore prose writing or even visual arts, employing the principles of concise expression you've honed through your tanka practice.

Don't limit yourself to the confines of a single form. Embrace the cross-pollination of ideas and techniques. The journey continues, not just in the realm of tanka, but in the broader landscape of creative expression. Your growth as a tanka writer will influence your other creative pursuits, creating a rich tapestry of artistic experience. Let the essence of tanka, its emphasis on precision and emotional depth, inform your entire creative process, coloring all your future endeavors. This is the lasting legacy of your tanka journey, a refined sensitivity to language and a deepened understanding of the world within and around you.

Engage with other poets, attend workshops, join online communities, participate in contests. Share your work, seek feedback, and learn from the experiences of others. The poetic community is a vibrant ecosystem, offering support, inspiration, and a platform for growth. This collective engagement is crucial to pushing your boundaries and understanding the evolution of the art form. Remember that your journey isn't a solitary one. It's enriched by the presence of others.

Remember the initial excitement, the thrill of discovery as you first began to craft your own tanka. Cultivate that sense of wonder, that passion for the craft. Let it fuel your ongoing exploration and propel you towards even greater heights in your poetic journey. Continue to nurture your creativity, to challenge your assumptions, and to embrace the transformative power of language.

This ongoing process of refinement is a testament to your dedication and a reflection of your evolving self. Embrace the journey, not just as a quest for mastery of a form, but as a journey of personal growth and artistic self-discovery. This continuous evolution is the heart of your creative journey, constantly pushing and inspiring you to explore new realms of artistry. The journey is, ultimately, about the process as much as the product, about the constant growth and refinement of both your skills and your spirit.

7.1 Growth & Refinement

Your initial exploration of tanka likely focused on mastering the form itself—the syllable count, the kigo, the precise placement of images. Now, consider this: technical proficiency is merely the foundation. True artistry lies in the subtle nuances, the emotional resonance that elevates your work beyond mere technical correctness. Growth, in the world of tanka, isn't just about writing more poems; it's about deepening the emotional current flowing through each line.

Think of your tanka as a delicate bonsai tree. Initially, you carefully shaped its branches, ensuring the correct structure. Now, it's time for the ongoing care – the subtle pruning, the careful nurturing that allows the tree to flourish and reveal its unique beauty. Refinement, in this context, involves a constant process of reviewing, revising, and rediscovering the emotional core of your work. Don't be afraid to revisit older poems, looking for ways to sharpen imagery, strengthen rhythm, or deepen the emotional impact. Sometimes, a single word change can transform a poem from adequate to exceptional.

Revisiting past work allows for a fresh perspective. Time provides distance, allowing you to see your poems with clearer eyes. You might discover underlying themes you hadn't fully grasped initially. Perhaps a poem written in a rush reveals a powerful emotion that deserves more exploration. This process of revisiting and refining will enrich your understanding of your own emotional landscape and how effectively you translate it into tanka.

It's a cyclical process; you write, you revise, you learn, and you write again, each iteration building on the last. This iterative approach is key to your growth.

The journey of refining your tanka isn't solitary. Engage with the wider community of tanka poets. Seek feedback from trusted readers – writers who understand the nuances of the form. Constructive criticism can illuminate areas needing improvement, whether it's sharpening the imagery, refining the word choice, or clarifying the poem's emotional core. However, remember to discern between genuine feedback and subjective opinions. Your artistic vision should remain paramount. Remember, the goal is to refine your craft, not to conform to external expectations.

Consider the impact of your chosen kigo. Does it truly enhance the emotional core of your tanka, or is it merely decorative? Often, less is more in tanka. A single, powerfully evocative image can speak volumes, while too much imagery can dilute the poem's impact, obscuring the central emotion. Strive for economy of language, yet retain the emotional depth. Every word should contribute meaningfully to the poem's overall impact; unnecessary words are distractions from its true essence.

As you refine your craft, you'll naturally develop a unique voice – a distinctive style that sets your work apart. Embrace experimentation. Don't be afraid to break the rules occasionally, so long as you do so consciously, with a deep understanding of the impact these choices might have on the poem's emotional resonance. While respecting the traditional form, find ways to imbue your tanka with personal expression, allowing your unique perspective and emotional experiences to shine through. It's in these nuances that your true artistry will blossom.

Beyond the technical aspects, focus on the emotional arc of your tanka. Does the poem effectively convey a complete emotional journey? Do the images selected and the language used enhance this journey? Aim to evoke a specific feeling or mood in the reader—a sense of awe, sadness, joy, or longing. The effectiveness of your tanka is measured by the emotional impact it leaves on the reader. And that impact comes from skillful selection of words, images, and careful attention to the underlying emotion. The most moving tankas leave a lasting impression.

Finally, remember that growth in tanka, like any artistic pursuit, is a lifelong journey. It's about continuous learning, constant refinement, and a relentless pursuit of emotional depth. Embrace the challenges, celebrate your successes, and never stop exploring the infinite possibilities within this concise yet profound poetic form. The more you practice, the more you revise, the more your voice will emerge and mature. And as your ability to craft these small poems develops, so will your ability to tell deeper stories. The journey never ends; it simply deepens and evolves. The tanka is more than just a structure. It's a path of emotional exploration and expression.

7.2 Beyond the Tanka

The concise beauty of the tanka, its ability to capture a fleeting moment or a profound emotion in just thirty-one syllables, can feel intensely satisfying. However, your journey as a poet doesn't end there. The discipline and focus honed through tanka writing become invaluable tools, transferable skills ready to enrich your expression in other poetic forms.

Consider the haiku, the tanka's shorter cousin. You've already mastered the art of concise imagery and precise word choice within a strict structure. Applying this knowledge to the haiku's seventeen syllables will feel natural, a comfortable expansion rather than a daunting leap. Experiment with juxtapositions, mirroring the techniques you've employed in your tankas to create surprising and meaningful connections within the haiku's tighter confines.

Moving beyond the fixed-form world opens up thrilling possibilities. Free verse, with its liberated structure, might seem initially overwhelming after the structured discipline of the tanka. Yet, the core skills remain vital. Your ability to select powerful, evocative words, to construct lines that resonate with rhythm and internal rhyme, will seamlessly translate. Free verse allows for longer explorations of theme, a richer tapestry of imagery, but the precision cultivated through tanka remains essential. Don't abandon the careful crafting; use it as the foundation for a more expansive expression.

The techniques you've mastered can even enhance your prose writing. Imagine the impact of weaving short, powerful sentences – the essence of the tanka – into your narrative, to create moments of heightened intensity or emotional clarity. Consider how carefully chosen words, honed through your tanka practice, lend a distinct voice and style to your prose. The concision, the focus on precise imagery, the power of suggestion rather than explicit statement – these are strengths that will elevate your writing in any form.

Beyond poetry and prose, the benefits extend to other creative realms. Think about songwriting. The structural discipline of the tanka mirrors the structure of a song, with its verses and refrains. The skill in crafting evocative imagery translates directly to crafting powerful lyrics. Consider the concision of a tanka: that very same skill allows for impactful song writing where each word must count.

Furthermore, the contemplative nature of tanka writing can inform other artistic endeavors. The careful observation required to capture a scene or emotion in a few lines enhances your powers of observation in visual art, painting, or photography. Consider that the process of refining a tanka, eliminating unnecessary words and enhancing the impact of each remaining word, is a process similar to editing a photograph or film.

The journey, then, isn't merely about mastering the tanka, but about uncovering the potential it unlocks. The refined sensitivity, the meticulous attention to detail, the ability to express profound emotion through economy of language – these are gifts that transcend the form itself. Embrace the newfound possibilities, allowing the skills you've nurtured to shape your creative expression in ways you may not have yet imagined. The tanka's tender touch may have begun your creative journey, but it is far from the destination. The path ahead stretches wide, waiting to be explored. The world is brimming with untold stories waiting to be shaped by the tools you have already acquired; don't let them go to waste.

www.ingramcontent.com/pod-product-compliance
Lightning Source LLC
LaVergne TN
LVHW020054090126
829337LV00065B/1283